YOGA FOR CHILDREN

YOGA FOR

CHILDREN

by Erene Cheki Haney and Ruth Richards

illustrated by Betty Schilling

The Bobbs-Merrill Company, Inc.
Indianapolis   New York

The Bobbs-Merrill Company, Inc.
Publishers   Indianapolis   New York
Text copyright © 1973 by Erene Cheki Haney and Ruth Richards
Illustrations copyright © 1973 by Betty Schilling
Design by Jack Jaget
Printed in the United States of America
ISBN 0-672-51801-5
Library of Congress catalog card number 73-1758
0 9 8 7 6 5 4 3 2 1

INTRODUCTION

Centuries ago the sages of India, observing the supple bodies and perpetual good health of the animals, imitated their movements and discovered that many of their bending and stretching motions were beneficial for the human body. These yogis developed a system of postures, or exercises, that are both isometric (tensing) and isotonic (stretching).

Ancient as the system is, yoga endures to this day and is practiced the world over to increase physical fitness and mental alertness. In a popular rediscovery of yoga principles, modern acrobatics, calisthenics, and dance have borrowed heavily from this system of exercise.

Here is a group of yoga postures that have been used successfully in special yoga classes for children, who delight in imitating animals. In the process of learning to perform these exercises smoothly, the child will develop his power of concentration. The "coming out" stage of the positions will teach him how to relax. These skills are valuable in adolescence and on into adult life.

Parents and other adults will find that they too derive benefits from practicing these postures with the children.

Teachers who use physical-movement games in the classroom will find the postures particularly useful. The animal games can help to calm an over-stimulated class. Children who are restless from too much sitting will find a new focus for their attention. When writing and other tedious desk work cause young backs to tire, shoulders to slump and arm and finger muscles to cramp, these exercises will release tensions and brighten spirits. They give free rein to the imagination, and they are fun to do.

Sequence of Postures

1.	Rabbit	9.	Deer
2.	Frog	10.	Butterfly
3.	Cat	11.	Lion
4.	Camel	12.	Cobra
5.	Rooster	13.	Grasshopper
6.	Stork	14.	Fish
7.	Eagle	15.	Swan
8.	Monkey	16.	Sponge

The sequence of postures is designed to permit an easy flow from one posture to the next and to allow the child to exercise each part of the body separately.

The first posture, the rabbit, provides a gentle stretch for the arms and shoulders. This is followed by the frog, a leg posture. The cat and the camel are complete exercises in themselves as they stretch the spine first in one direction and then in another.

The rooster, the stork and the eagle are balance postures. Equally important, they are also concentration exercises. All three involve tensing of the leg and foot muscles for toning and muscle control. The eagle, the most difficult of the three, requires control of the entire body.

The monkey posture follows, to limber up the backs of the legs.

The deer provides another stretch for the arms and shoulders, the butterfly for the legs. Tensing for the lion stimulates circulation in the eye, ear and throat areas.

The cobra and the grasshopper are primarily for the lower back. The fish, which follows, is for the upper back and neck. The swan will relieve any tension in the shoulders and is a good stretch to finish with.

The final posture, the sponge, is for complete relaxation and should never be neglected when practicing yoga. This is the expansion after the contraction, the principle upon which yoga exercises are based. This is why one feels so refreshed after a yoga workout.

Certain postures serve particular parts of the body. The sixteen given here work the entire body from head to toe. However, it is not necessary to use all sixteen at once. If time is limited, the body can receive a good overall workout from a few carefully chosen postures. Two suggested shorter routines follow:

Rabbit	Deer
Cat	Camel
Rooster	Stork
Eagle	Monkey
Butterfly	Frog
Lion	Lion
Cobra	Grasshopper
Fish	Fish
Swan	Swan
Sponge	Sponge

Things to Remember When Practicing Yoga

☐ There is never any competition in yoga, either with the instructor or with another child. Competition creates tension. Do the best you can. That is enough.

☐ If you are exercising with others, pay no attention to them. Act as though you were alone in the room.

☐ Be relaxed. Move relaxed. Rest relaxed. Move slowly into and out of the position. Not S—L—O—W—L—Y, but S-L-O-W-L-Y.

like this

☐ When sitting, keep head and neck in a straight line.

like this

☐ When bending forward or rising up again, do not move head separately. Move in one smooth motion, using the back (spine) to bring you forward or back.

☐ NEVER STRAIN
In doing postures that call for your head to move backward, never put it so far back as to strain your neck.

☐ Always end each exercise with a few moments of rest. A slow count of ten to fifteen is suggested. Resting postures follow.

Positions for Resting

In each case, eyes are closed; body is relaxed.

When you are standing, arms hang easily at the sides.

When you are lying down, arms are away from the body; palms are up. Legs are slightly apart; toes face each other; heels fall to the sides.

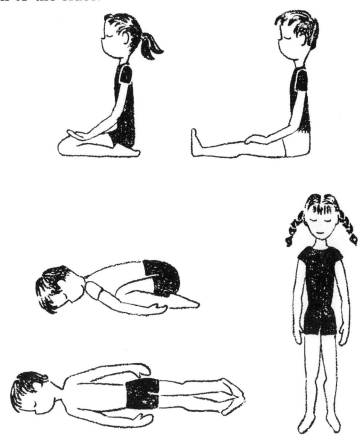

AND NOW TO BEGIN:

I am a **rabbit** resting with ears folded back.

How to Do It   # The Rabbit

☐ Sit on your heels. Reach back and hold your heels.

☐ Still holding your heels, bend forward S-L-O-W-L-Y.

☐ Place the top of your head on the floor, close to your knees. Now rise up off your heels. Count to 5.

☐ S-L-O-W-L-Y sit up.

☐ Place your hands on your thighs, palms up. Sit with your back and your head in a straight line, and REST.

I am a **frog.** I sit quietly, blinking my eyes and breathing softly.

☐ Sit on your heels. Place your hands on your thighs.

☐ Spread your knees far apart and try to touch your toes in back. (Sit firmly on the floor and not on your heels.)

☐ In this position count to 5.

☐ Bring your knees together again and sit on your heels.

I am a **cat** crouching before I pounce.

How to Do It

Part 1

☐ Sit on your heels.

☐ Kneel.

☐ Spread your knees apart. Bend over and place your hands on the floor. (Hands and knees are apart, like the legs on a table.)

☐ Moving head and chest together, slowly lower chest and chin to the floor. Elbows will flare out as you come down. Count to 5.

☐ Now slowly, in one smooth motion, lift up your back like an angry cat, pull in your stomach, and let your head hang down easily.

☐ Relax your back; release your stomach.

☐ Then sit back on your heels.

The Cat

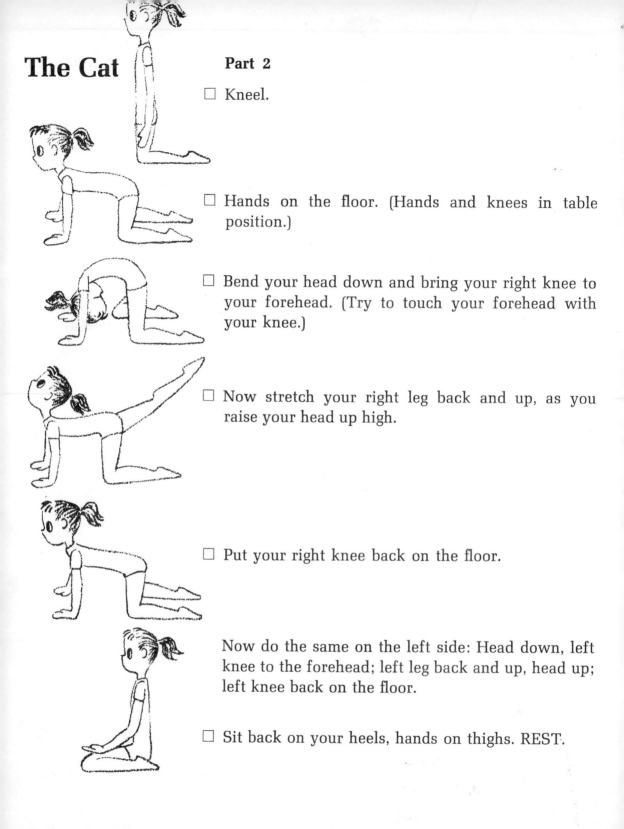

Part 2

☐ Kneel.

☐ Hands on the floor. (Hands and knees in table position.)

☐ Bend your head down and bring your right knee to your forehead. (Try to touch your forehead with your knee.)

☐ Now stretch your right leg back and up, as you raise your head up high.

☐ Put your right knee back on the floor.

Now do the same on the left side: Head down, left knee to the forehead; left leg back and up, head up; left knee back on the floor.

☐ Sit back on your heels, hands on thighs. REST.

How to Do It

Part 1

The Camel

☐ Sit on your heels.

☐ Reach back and put your hands on the floor behind your feet. Lean back, letting your head hang easily. Count to 5.

☐ Come forward slowly and gracefully. Continue forward. Let your arms fall naturally at your sides; place forehead on the floor; REST. Count to 10.

☐ Come up slowly to sit on your heels.

Part 2

Now try it this way:

☐ Sit on your heels.

☐ Put your hands on the floor behind your feet.

☐ Lean back, raise your hips, and let your head hang back easily. Count to 5.

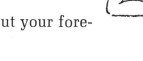

☐ Come forward slowly and gracefully; put your forehead on the floor; REST. Count to 10.

I am a **camel.** I stretch backwards after carrying a heavy load.

The Camel

☐ Come up slowly to sit on your heels.

When you have practiced the first two stages of the camel posture long enough and can do them easily, try this:

Part 3

☐ Sit on your heels.

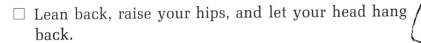

☐ Hands on the floor, behind your feet.

☐ Lean back, raise your hips, and let your head hang back.

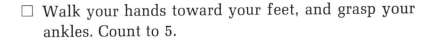

☐ Walk your hands toward your feet, and grasp your ankles. Count to 5.

☐ To get up, put your weight on your right arm. Then lift your left arm above your head and come up slowly to straighten your body.

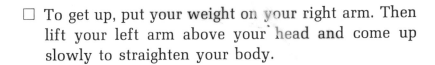

☐ Slowly come forward; put your forehead on the floor; REST. Count to 10.

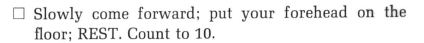

I am a **rooster** greeting the sun with outstretched wings.

How to Do It

The Rooster

☐ Stand up straight.

☐ Breathe in as you slowly rise up on your toes and stretch your arms out at the sides.

☐ Hold your breath for a moment and balance on your toes.

☐ Breathe out slowly as you lower your arms to your sides and come down on your heels.

☐ REST for a moment with your eyes closed. Open your eyes and try this again.

I am a silent **stork** standing on one leg.

How to Do It

☐ Stand straight, with your arms at your sides. Arms are relaxed, not stiff. Stare straight ahead at some point on the wall.

☐ Put all your weight on the right leg. Bend your left knee and lift your foot, toes pointing toward the floor.

☐ Bending your left elbow, raise your forearm to waist level, fingers pointing toward the floor. Balance to the count of 6.

☐ Lower your foot and arm at the same time; relax your eyes; REST.

Now try this standing on your left leg.

I am a proud **eagle** balancing on a rock.

How to Do It

The Eagle

☐ Stand straight, putting all your weight on your right leg.

☐ Wrap your left leg around your right leg, and bend as if you were about to sit down.

☐ Wrap your right arm around your left arm.

☐ To make an eagle's beak, touch your nose with your finger. Count to 5.

☐ Gently unlock arms and legs and come out of the posture S-L-O-W-L-Y and with control. (Don't fly out.) Straighten your arms and legs.

☐ Stand tall to REST.

Do the same posture standing on your left leg.

I am a **monkey** walking on the forest floor.

How to Do It

The Monkey

□ Stand up straight.

□ Keeping your legs straight, bend over and touch the floor. Put your hands flat on the floor.

□ Now, looking straight ahead, walk like a monkey. Walk around the room and back to your starting place.

□ Keeping your legs straight, come up slowly to a standing position.

□ Stand straight, but relaxed, and REST.

I am a **fawn** stretching my neck this way and that.

How to Do It

The Deer

- ☐ Sit with your legs straight in front of you.

- ☐ Put your left foot under your right thigh.

- ☐ Bend your right knee and bring it close to your chest. Lean forward slightly and stretch your arms out in front of your knee.

- ☐ Separate your arms and bring your hands around to the back. Clasp your hands in back. Look up and over your left shoulder. Count to 5.

- ☐ Unclasp your hands and slowly unwind.

- ☐ Put your legs straight out in front of you. Eyes closed; palms on knees. REST for a moment.

Now try this with your right foot under your left thigh.

I am a **butterfly.** I fan my wings to make them strong.

How to Do It

☐ Sit with a straight back.

☐ Bring the soles of your feet together.

☐ Clasp your hands under your feet. Stretch tall.

☐ Holding your feet in place, gently move your knees up and down. Flutter them as if they were wings.

☐ Bring legs out straight and REST.

I am a **lion,** making a face and looking fierce.

How to Do It

The Lion

☐ Sit on your heels. Place your hands on your knees, palms down.

☐ Stiffen your arms and back as a lion does when he is ready to pounce.

☐ Make your fingers straight and stiff. Open your eyes wide and look up. Now stick out your tongue!

☐ Hold this position for the count of 5.

☐ Relax your whole body and sit back naturally. REST for a moment with your hands on your thighs and your eyes closed.

I am a **cobra** rising up slowly, one vertebra at a time.

How to Do It

The Cobra

☐ Lie on your stomach with your forehead touching the floor, your feet together.

☐ Place your hands flat on the floor under your shoulders, fingers pointing forward. Keep your elbows close to your sides.

☐ Now lift your head, bringing your chin forward to touch the floor.

☐ Eyes wide open, looking up, slowly raise your head and chest.

☐ Press down with your hands and continue to bend back from the waist, keeping your hips on the floor. Elbows are slightly bent. Look up at the ceiling. Count to 5.

☐ S-L-O-W-L-Y come down. Waist first to the floor, then chest, then chin. Now forehead to floor.

☐ Turn your cheek to the floor; REST.

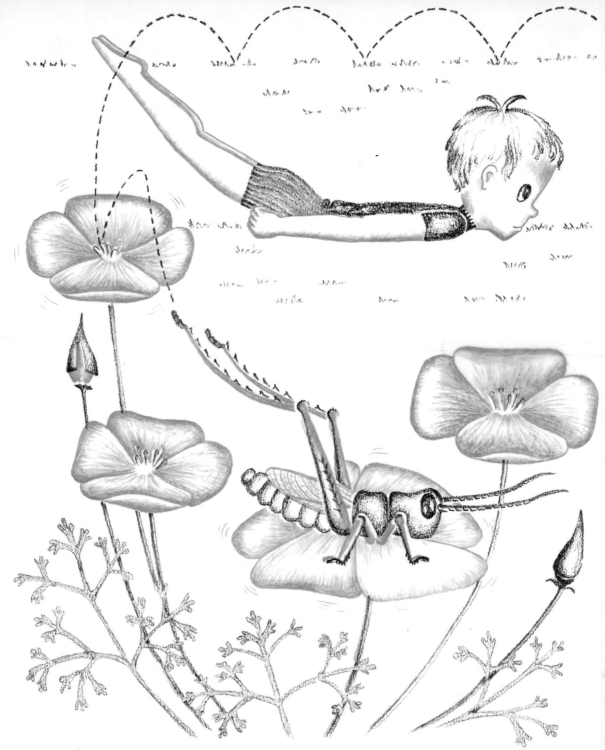

I am a **grasshopper.** With strong legs I jump from one flower to another.

How to Do It   Little Grasshopper

- [ ] Lie on your stomach with your arms at your sides. Legs together, chin on the floor.

- [ ] Make two fists, thumbs touching the floor. Place fists close to thighs.

- [ ] Now, all at the same time: take a deep breath, push down on the floor with your fists, and raise your left leg.

- [ ] Count to 3.

- [ ] Now as you breathe out S-L-O-W-L-Y, bring your leg down.

- [ ] Open fists; relax. Put your cheek on the floor; REST.

Then make two fists, place them close to the thighs, and try this on the other side, breathing in, pushing down on your fists and raising the right leg.

Big Grasshopper

- [ ] Start the same way, chin on the floor and arms at your sides. Make fists.

- [ ] Now, as you breathe in, push down on fists and slowly raise both legs together.

- [ ] Count to 3.

- [ ] As you breathe out, slowly lower both legs together.

- [ ] Relax arms and legs, put your cheek on the floor, and REST.

I am a **fish** curving my back as I swim.

How to Do It   **The Fish**

- [ ] Sit on your heels and place your hands on the floor behind you. Lean back.

- [ ] Let your hands walk forward until your elbows touch the floor.

- [ ] Gently let your head fall back until it rests on the floor.

- [ ] When you are firmly balanced on your head, remove your hands from the floor. Bring your palms together over your chest.

- [ ] Count to 5.

- [ ] Place your elbows on the floor. Use them for support and gently raise yourself up.

- [ ] Bend forward, forehead on the floor; REST.

I am a graceful **swan.**

How to Do It

The Swan

☐ Sit on your heels.

☐ Put your forehead on the floor. Stretch your arms out in front of you as far as they will go.

☐ Keep your hands and feet where they are and come up on your hands and knees, arms straight.

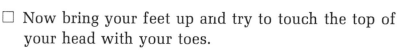

☐ Stretch your body forward. Hold your head back.

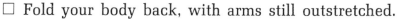

☐ Now bring your feet up and try to touch the top of your head with your toes.

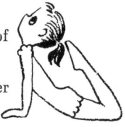

☐ Keep hands and knees in place as you slowly lower your legs.

☐ Fold your body back, with arms still outstretched.

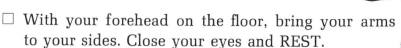

☐ With your forehead on the floor, bring your arms to your sides. Close your eyes and REST.

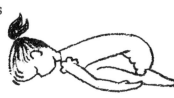

I am a soft **sponge** living at the bottom of the sea.

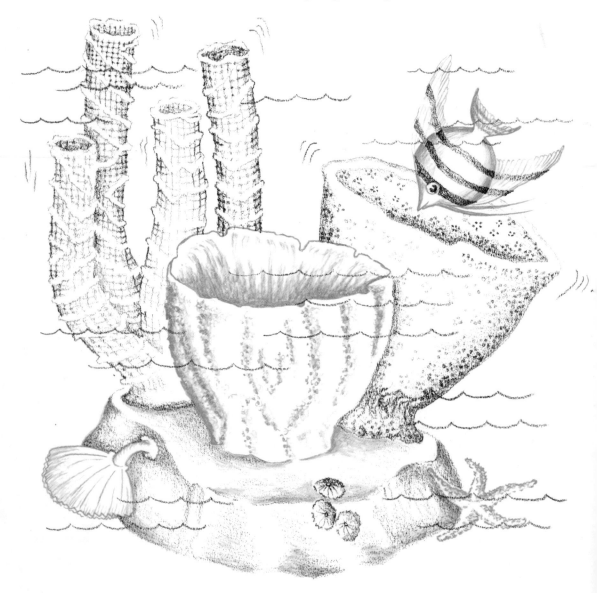

The Sponge

You have been busy pretending to be all these animals. Did you know that a sponge, which lives in the sea, is also an animal?

In this yoga posture we relax like a sponge.

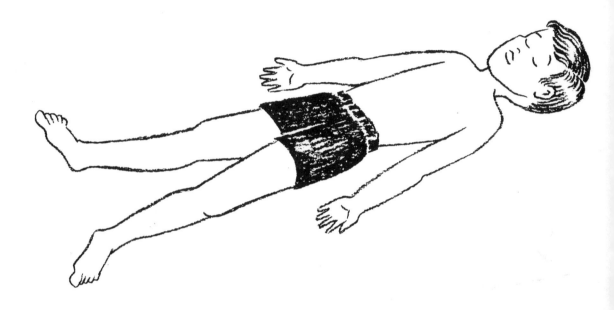

How to Do It

☐ Lie on your back with your arms at your sides. Palms are up. Eyes closed. Legs are slightly apart, feet falling to the sides.

☐ Let your whole body, from your toes to your head, sink into the floor.

Think of a sponge, deep down in the sea. Lie in this relaxed position for 2 minutes.